How to Get More Love

50 Insights into the Opposite Sex

Karen Card
Relationship Expert

Published by
KarCom LLC
P.O. Box 4887
Clearwater, FL 33758-4887
(727) 512-2899
www.CoachingForLove.com

Table of Contents

INSIGHTS INTO COMMUNICATION

INSIGHTS INTO DATING

INSIGHTS INTO RELATIONSHIPS

Dedication

This book is dedicated to the love of my life,
my husband Stan.

Thanks for all your love and support

.

Introduction

FOR SINGLES AND COUPLES....

When I started my Relationship Coaching business, I was very anxious to help as many people as possible improve their love lives. What I found was a lot of people whose lives were too busy to slow down and learn how to be successful in their relationships. I wanted to teach people exactly what to do to get love, but most did not have the time to learn. This is when I began sending out bits of information in my weekly relationship tips. By giving people a small dose of knowledge on a weekly basis, they were able to take in what I wanted to teach.

After many months of emailing Weekly Relationship Insights, and numerous requests from new subscribers for previous tips, I decided it was time to put the tips into a book.

I hope you enjoy "How to Get More Love," and that you learn what you need to be successful in love.

Insights into the Differences between Men & Women

Insight #1:

Do You Want Romance or Equality?

For an intimate relationship to be healthy, it needs to be balanced. Balanced does not mean the same as "equal" in a relationship. A "balanced" relationship means each person gives their "good stuff" to the other, but it is not the SAME good stuff. For example, a man may give his "service" (fixing a broken computer), while a woman may give her "appreciation" (thanking and praising him). Whereas in an "equal" relationship, both partners contribute exactly the same, i.e. each paying 50% of the dining out costs.

While society tells us that "equality" is good, it is not the way to sustain a romantic relationship - it is actually the description of a BUSINESS partnership. Ask yourself, "Do I want a romantic relationship or do I want a 50-50 business/roommate situation?"

A healthy romantic relationship requires balance between the role of the man and the woman in order to create chemistry and intimacy. Men need to feel respected and appreciated and women need to feel cared for and cherished. This doesn't happen when each partner is "going Dutch" on a date.

Advice to Men

Do not expect her to pay half (even if she offers). You are the masculine partner and therefore you should be paying for dates and she should be giving you her "good stuff," which is appreciation and respect.

Advice to Women

Do not ask him out or offer to pay half on a date. His "good stuff" is showing you a nice time and your "good stuff" is appreciation with a smile and kind words. A woman should only offer to pay half at business meetings, not on dates.

Insight #2:

Asking for Directions

Why won't he stop and ask for directions? Because he is a man.

The main reason men do not like asking for directions is because they have a strong belief that they can "do it on their own." Men believe if they are lost, they will be able to find their way out, on their own, without needing help from anyone. Where women are willing to ask for and receive help from anyone (even gas station clerks), men feel their intellect is being challenged if they have to ask for help. Men associate their value as a person with their ability to figure things out on their own.

From *The Guy Rules*: Christopher Columbus did NOT need directions and neither do we.

Advice to Men

When you are with a woman and she suggests you ask for directions, do not think of it as an insult. Think of it as another way you can make her happy. You will be getting the directions just to make her happy, and not because you couldn't figure it out on your own.

Advice to Women

Next time you are with a man and you are lost, stay calm and try not to offer advice. Try to relax and enjoy the scenery. Give him a chance to figure it out on his own (you could even give him support with this). If that does not work, ask him if he would be willing to stop so you can go in and get the directions. Whatever you do, do not make him feel bad that you are lost.

Insight #3:

Are you a Waffle or Spaghetti?

Why is it so hard to figure out the opposite sex? Because our brains work differently.

Men's brains are really good at focusing completely on just one thought and women's brains are really good at thinking many thoughts at the same time. This difference can make it hard to figure out what each other is thinking.

To illustrate this, picture a waffle. A waffle has many squares, each divided by little walls high enough to hold syrup. This is an example of a man's brain. Each waffle square is a thought or idea. In order for a man to change from one idea to the next, he needs to get out of the square he is in and climb over the wall to get into the next idea.

Now picture a plate of spaghetti. This is an example of a woman's brain. Each spaghetti noodle is one thought or idea. However, each thought (noodle) is touching about seven other thoughts (noodles) at the same time. Women are regularly thinking at least seven thoughts at the same time.

Understanding how our brains work differently will help improve our communication with the opposite sex.

Advice to Men

When she asks you to do a task, and then asks you to do 3 other tasks at the same time, remember that this is just how her brain works. Each thought is touching seven other thoughts. Remind her that your brain works better when you can focus completely on one task at a time.

Advice to Women

Knowing how his brain is different should keep you from getting so mad at him when he is slow to change his attention from the TV to you. Give him time to move into a new waffle square when you need him to change his focus or thoughts toward you.

Insight #4:

Is Competition Healthy?

It is natural for a man to want to compete. Whether he is at work, driving his car, or on the golf course, competition is just what men do. It is what makes them feel good about themselves.

Competition is generally a masculine trait, and it is normal for women to be masculine <u>at work</u>; everyone is masculine at work. However, if she is masculine (competitive) at home or in social situations, she is damaging her romantic relationship.

When a woman competes with her partner, he will see her as another competitor and will want to win at any cost. Even though he may love her very much, once the competition begins, he will not be concerned with her feelings – he will only be focused on the competition and winning.

Advice to Men

Unless you are business rivals, stop competing with her. Even if she talks/acts masculine, avoid the competition. In a healthy relationship, a man cares for and respects a woman; he does not set out to prove he is better than she is.

Advice to Women

Ask yourself, do you want to compete with your man or do you want to be cherished and cared for? While it may feel normal to want to compete, it will feel even better when you stop the competition and let him care for you. Proving to him you are better will <u>not</u> make him love you more.

Insight #5:

Men, Don't Give Solutions

Men want to help solve problems in order to feel useful – especially the problems of their significant others.

When a woman talks, with the intention of sharing her feelings, it can sound to a man as if she is describing a problem to him that he needs to solve. Because he cares about her, he wants to solve her problems (thinking this will make her happy). Unfortunately, as she is discussing her negative feelings and needing him to just listen; he is giving her directions on what she should do to fix things. A woman may interpret his solutions as him invalidating her feelings. She doesn't want advice, just reassurance that her feelings are normal. She wants to hear that it is okay to be mad at her boss.

Although his intentions are good, the result is that she feels like he is not really listening and doesn't really care for her.

Advice to Men

Learn to just listen – without giving advice. Realize when she wants to talk, she is not looking for solutions. A woman can solve her negative feelings just by talking about them with someone who will listen to her and validate her feelings.

Advice to Women

Understand he has the best intentions - making you happy. Start your conversations by saying, "I'd like to talk, would you mind just listening?" You may need to occasionally remind him throughout the conversation that you appreciate his solutions, but you really just need him to listen. Listening without problem-solving is not natural for most men, so don't get mad if he isn't able to do this immediately.

Insight #6:

Asking for Help

If a woman asks a man for help, he feels good. The request makes him feel important and he wants to help her. The more a man can successfully help a woman, the more he is attracted to her. He feels like her "Knight in Shining Armor."

However, a woman wanting to return the favor and offering to help a man will not get the same result. Unless HE specifically ASKS for her help, he may be insulted and feel that her unsolicited help or advice is implying he's unable to do it himself. Men like to solve their own problems. They feel smart when they can figure things out on their own. That's why men don't like to stop to ask for directions.

Advice to Men

Realize a woman may offer to help you only because she wants you to feel good about her (she thinks she's helping and you will be appreciative), not because she doesn't trust you to do it on your own. To avoid hurt feelings, you can gently tell her you would really prefer to do things yourself.

Advice to Women

It's very important to avoid offering a man unsolicited help or advice – he usually doesn't want it and will NOT value it. Alternately, don't worry about being "needy" if you ask a man for his help. He will enjoy the appreciation you give him for his help in getting the job done.

Insight #7:

How Was Your Day?

When he asks her, "How was your day?" she can talk for twenty minutes. She can tell him about every major event that happened and even some minor events, if she remembers them. Depending on her mood, she will tell him all the bad stuff, most of the good stuff and some of the in-between stuff. Women feel good when they can talk in great detail about their day.

When she asks him, "How was your day?" he answers, "Fine." And he is done talking. His answer was direct, to the point, and in his mind adequately answered the question that was asked. Now he wants to get focused back on whatever task or project is currently the priority on his mind.

Men have the ability to focus all their energy on one thing, whereas women tend to continually focus on ten things at once. This difference in focus leads to men answering questions directly and without detail, and women answering questions indirectly and in great detail. Neither way is right or wrong, they are just different and we need to accept it.

Advice to Men

Learn to listen. She is not asking you to solve the day's problems. All she needs is for you to look at her while she is talking, give her a sympathetic nod, a few "uh-huhs" and she will feel you really care about her.

Advice to Women

Accept this difference between men and women and do not take it personally if he doesn't talk in great detail. It does not mean he doesn't want to share his day with you; he is just being direct.

Insight #8:

A Man with a Plan

To keep a healthy balance of masculine and feminine energy in a relationship, the man needs to make most of the decisions with the woman having the final say of yes or no. Instead of him saying to her, "What do you think we should do?" he should say, "I think we should do this or do that, how do you feel about it?" Then the woman answers with a yes or no.

Women love a man with a plan. This interaction allows the man to be masculine and make the initial plan, and allows the woman to feel respected and cared for by having the last say in the decision.

Advice to Men

Instead of asking her if she wants to go out this weekend, have a plan in mind and tell her you would like to take her to _____ (a movie, dancing, etc.) and then ask her how she feels about it. If she says no, have a Plan B in mind. She will appreciate your effort of planning ahead.

Advice to Women

Let him make some decisions. It really does feel good to sit back, relax and not have to think of all the details. Let him do this for you and enjoy being cared for.

Insight #9:

How do You Handle Stress?

How do you react when you're stressed? A masculine-energy person (usually a man), will go inside himself (in his head) to think about the problem and come up with a solution. A feminine-energy person (usually a woman), will need to talk about the problem to come up with a solution. Neither technique is right or wrong – they're just very different. This difference in the processing of stress can cause a big problem in relationships when we don't recognize what our partner is doing.

If he needs quiet time to think (in his head), and she continues to ask him questions about what is wrong, he will feel attacked (not supported) and will end up feeling more stress. If she needs to talk and he can't listen or give her the attention she needs (because he is inside himself), then she feels even more stress.

Advice to Men

When a woman is feeling stressed, help her out by listening to her talk. This does not mean giving her advice (even though this is your natural response); it means listening, acknowledging and validating her feelings while she talks it out. This is how you can help her get through her stress.

Advice to Women

When a man is feeling stress, leave him alone until he is ready to talk. Women need to practice this technique of giving him space and not taking it personally if he doesn't want to talk. Even though 'talking it out' is her natural response, talking is not going to help him when he needs to be in his head.

Insight #10:

Complaining or Sharing?

Most women "share" their thoughts and feelings as a way to process stress. Unfortunately for women, sharing can sound like complaining to men. When a problem has no solution, men tend to avoid talking about it. If they cannot fix it, why bother discussing it. Women, however, talk about their problems and frustrations as a way to release tension. Women share their negative feelings looking to get empathy and understanding, which immediately makes them feel better.

Men do not normally share their feelings; because of this, most men cannot tell the difference between a woman complaining and a woman sharing. Due to this lack of understanding, men tend to react to a woman's sharing – what he hears as complaining – with a negative or judgmental reaction. This basic male response is the opposite of what a woman wants and can actually cause her more stress.

Advice to Men

You can get ahead at work or at home if you can understand that when a woman is sharing, she would like you to listen with concern and empathy. If she feels heard and understood you will earn her trust and respect.

Advice to Women

When you share or vent to a man, preface the conversation with, "I'm not complaining, I just need to vent for a few minutes, do you have time to listen?" That way he can recognize that you are not complaining and giving him more problems to solve. This lead-in allows him to listen to you without a negative reaction.

Insight #11:

He Forgot My Birthday

Men sometimes forget important dates; not because they are mean or do not care, but because they are men. Men do not <u>want</u> to forget, because they do not want make her upset. However, men tend to be single focused and they are usually focused on projects or tasks and not calendar dates. When men are stressed, they get even more focused, whereas women remember every detail and then some.

Unlike women, men do not usually buy other men birthday cards, and they are rarely offended if another guy forgets their birthday. Celebrating holidays is much more important to women than it is to most men. Women will need to remind men of upcoming important dates (her birthday or anniversary). He will actually appreciate the reminder.

Advice to Men

You need to accept the fact that holidays are important to women, even if it seems silly to you. Make sure you put her birthday and your anniversary on your calendar (both work and personal calendars). Do not forget – or you will lose many, many points.

Advice to Women

<u>Remind him</u> of upcoming important dates! It does not prove he does not love you enough if he forgets - do not let him forget. It is okay to make a huge deal of your birthday or anniversary and start giving him reminders about one month out, and then at two weeks out, then two days, etc.

Men really do want to make women happy, and letting him forget your birthday or anniversary does not make either of you happy.

Insight #12:

The Need to be Needed

Men need to be needed. It makes a man feel strong and confident when he is with a woman who needs him. He wants to do things for her, add value to her life and be the direct cause of her happiness. This is what makes a man feel good.

For some women, needing a man is a difficult concept. Many strong, independent women (including single moms) pride themselves on <u>not</u> needing a man. In fact, our society promotes the belief that a woman should be so independent that she will never need a man to take care of her. While being financially independent is a good thing, being so independent that she never lets a man do things for her is a bad thing. While she is trying to be strong and independent, he is trying to take care of her and they are both getting frustrated.

Advice to Men

Realize it is society that has made women feel it is wrong to need you. Explain to her it makes you feel good to do things for her and take care of her. When she resists your help, just reassure her that you know she can do it on her own, but because you care about her you want to make things easier for her.

Advice to Women

If you want true love from a man, you will need to change your beliefs – needing a man is not wrong. However being "needy" (clingy, desperate) is a turn-off.

Let him know you need him, and be receptive to his offers to help you. Let him do things for you – which makes him feel good about himself – and in the end you will reap the benefits.

Insight #13:

Head vs. Heart

When we are thinking, concentrating or focused on a project we are "in our heads." Our energy is coming from our head (our mind) and our actions are dictated by our focused thoughts.

When we are feeling emotions, caring for others, loving others and ourselves, we are "in our hearts." Our energy is coming from our heart and our actions are dictated by our feelings and love.

During the workday, men and women need to be "in their heads" to be successful. However, when women come home, they need to convert back to being "in their hearts" to really feel good. When a woman stays in her head and tries to care for her family, she feels anxiety. Using thoughts instead of feelings to care for a needy child or partner is frustrating and sometimes overwhelming.

Advice to Men

If you feel disconnected from your partner, it may be because she is stuck in her head and unable to give her love. Try to get her out of her head and back in her heart by taking care of her feelings. Talk about non-work issues she feels passionate about such as hobbies or upcoming vacation plans, or give her a shoulder or foot massage, or suggest she take 20 minutes to relax and unwind to help get her back into her heart.

Advice to Women

Try to get out of your head on the way home from work. If driving gives you anxiety, wait until you are in your driveway then take several deep breaths and try to feel your feelings. By getting into your heart before you go into your house, you will be better able to care for yourself and your family.

Insight #14:

Holiday Priorities

It is Christmas time. She needs to wrap the gifts with perfectly coordinated ribbons, because they are for all her family. He needs to hang the outside lights with precision, because the neighbors will be making comments.

Let's face it, men and women have different priorities during the holidays. She may want to spend all day baking goodies for her coworkers and he wants to spend the day watching football. Neither sees the value in what the other is doing, but that is just part of being men and women. During the holidays, our male/female differences show up frequently with our different priorities. With all the extra stress involved in getting ready for the holidays, it is more important than ever that you talk to each other about your priorities. There is no need to yell or be sarcastic, just talk to each other, accept that you are different and show respect to each other. With good communication, the holidays truly can be a peaceful time of year.

Advice to Men

She will be putting in more effort than you will on many little details you may not feel are important. Give her as much support as you can. When she gets frustrated, assure her that her hard work is worth it and that the holidays will be wonderful.

Advice to Women

Do not judge his priorities just because they are different from yours. If you need his help with a holiday project, ask him if he has time, and then let him know how much you would appreciate his help. He does not need to understand "why" it is important to you; he just needs to know that it is important to you and that you will appreciate him when it is done.

Insight #15:

To Give or Not to Give (Gifts)?

Women love to receive gifts – ranging in size from a card to flowers to jewelry. When a woman receives a gift (of any size), it tells her he was thinking about her and wants to make her happy. Women love this! On the other hand, when a woman gives a gift to a man (other than Christmas and his birthday) he may feel uncomfortable. If it is early in their relationship, he may feel that she is expecting a level of emotional commitment from him that he is not ready to give. To a man, it can feel that she is trying to buy his love.

Another reason he may not like getting a gift is that she may have spent more money than he did, and now he feels inferior. Since most men do not appreciate gifts in the way women do, men should be the primary <u>gift givers</u> and women should be the appreciative <u>gift receivers</u>.

Advice to Men

Give her gifts often! Even a simple hand-written love note counts as a gift. It is not just about spending money. She likes getting gifts because she likes that you are thinking about her when you are not with her, and you spent your time and energy toward making her happy. She will love that you took the effort to get her something, so all gifts win you points.

Advice to Women

Resist the urge to buy a man a gift outside of the holidays. Giving him a gift will not have the desired effect – he will not appreciate and love you more for thinking of him. That is what he is supposed to be doing for you.

Insight #16:

Is that Question Offensive?

Has a man ever asked you, "Why are you still single?" or has a woman ever asked you, "Why do you drive such an old car?" Before you get offended, remember that men and women think and speak differently. What is offensive to a woman may be a perfectly innocent question if asked to a man.

Based on the communication differences between the sexes, you may want to get a better understanding of the motivation behind the question before you get offended. You can do this by replying to their question with a question, such as, "Why would you ask that?" If you get a non-defensive answer like, "I just wanted to get to know you better," then you can relax and be assured that no offense was meant. (Answering a personal question with a question works well with most nosy people).

Men and women regularly cause confusion with each other based on our different styles of communication. Try to avoid adding resentment to the confusion by first clarifying any questions that may sound out of line to you.

Advice to Men

Be aware that most women are sensitive to their marital status, motherhood status, and weight. Try to avoid questions in these areas – you do not want to insult her when you are just trying to be friendly.

Advice to Women

Be aware that most men are sensitive to their careers, cars and material possessions. You do not want him to think you are judging him when you are just trying to learn more about him.

Insights into
Communication

Insight #17:

Do You Drop Hints?

Often times when a woman needs something from a man, she will "gently" try to get her needs met. She does this by "dropping hints" about what she needs, hoping he will figure it out and give it to her. Example: Hint: "The grass is getting long" vs. Direct: "Please cut the grass today."

Since women communicate intuitively (gently) to other women, they feel it is rude to ask for things directly. This 'indirect' communication works with other women, but not with men.

Unfortunately for women, most men just don't hear "hints." It's not that they aren't listening; it's just that men communicate directly and they assume if she wants something, she'll directly ask for it. He may want to give her what she wants, but he does not know what she is asking for.

Advice to Men

Let her know it is okay (not rude) for her to directly
ask for what she wants. By her asking you directly, it
will be easier for you to make her happy.

Advice to Women

To avoid being disappointed, stop relying on hints
and ask directly for what you want! It will make it
easier for him to make you happy.

Insight #18:

How to Avoid Arguments

One of the best ways to avoid an argument is to assume your partner did NOT mean to hurt you. If there is a problem or disagreement, it is most likely caused by a <u>mis-communication</u>. A mis-communication is when you hear something differently than your partner intended when they spoke. This happens all the time when men and women speak with each other. For example, he says, "I'll be back in a couple hours" and what he meant was "I'll be back whenever I'm done and it might be 5 hours, so don't worry." However, what she heard him say was, "I'll be back in 2 hours and if I'm not back, you should worry or get mad." Keeping in mind this happens frequently, you can understand how mis-communication can result in arguments and hurt feelings.

The next time you have an argument, try to explain to the other person what you heard them say and see if it is really what they meant. You need to start by believing the other person never intended to hurt you.

Advice to Men

When she is upset with you, ask her what she <u>thinks</u> you said. You may be very surprised to hear that she heard a message much worse than you intended. Likewise, when you are upset with her, tell her what you heard her say to see if the real message got lost in the translation.

Advice to Women

When you get upset with him, before you start an argument tell him what you heard him say. If he agrees you heard his intended message, then you probably will have a disagreement, but more frequently, he will tell you he never said that. Ask for clarification on the actual message and you will find there is no more reason to be upset.

Insight #19:

Does He Interrupt You?

When men talk to other men, they often interrupt each other to make a point or with a relative comment. Because most men do this, they feel it is a normal way of communicating and do not get offended when they are interrupted. In fact, they may reply to the interruption by saying, "Good point," and then continue their discussion.

Women on the other hand, show each other respect by NOT interrupting when one of them is speaking. Most women feel it is impolite and disrespectful to interrupt. They save their "good points and relative comments" until the speaker is finished and has made her point.

This difference in communication styles between men and women can cause conflict. When a man interrupts a woman, she may feel he is being rude and that he was not really listening to her.

Advice to Men

Knowing that she feels it is disrespectful, try to avoid interrupting her when she is speaking. Save your comments until she is finished.

Advice to Women

Remember that interrupting is natural for men, so do not take it personally. Because men have different rules, you need to let them know in advance what it is you want. Try starting a conversation by saying, "Please give me a few minutes to explain this, and then I would like to hear your thoughts."

Insight #20:

What's Wrong? Nothing

When a woman is upset, a man may ask her, "What's wrong?" Her automatic response is to answer, "Nothing." But, what she is really feeling is, "I am mad and hurt. I need your help, but I don't know how to ask for it."

However, when she answers, "Nothing" the man hears her say, "Nothing is wrong, or maybe something is wrong, but I don't want to talk about it." So, he shows her respect (as he would to a man) by leaving her alone and acting as if nothing is wrong. Unfortunately, when he acts like nothing is wrong, it makes her feel worse.

Advice to Men

If she seems upset, she probably is upset. To help her feel better, start by gently asking her some questions. Ask her if there is something you can do to help her feel better, or it she just wants to talk about it. Sometimes just talking about a problem will help a woman solve it.

Advice to Women

When he asks, tell him directly what is wrong. Or, if being direct is too uncomfortable, tell him you are upset, but you are not able to talk about it right now and would he be available to talk in an hour. Women, you really need to practice being direct to get your man to hear you and give you what you need.

Insight #21:

How to Give Advice to a Man

Because men pride themselves on being able to figure things out on their own, it is insulting to men when a woman offers unsolicited advice on how to do something. While she is giving him advice with the intention of making the situation better (making him happy with her), it has the opposite effect and makes him feel resentful of her. So what is a woman to do? The first choice is to avoid giving him advice, if possible. If this is not possible, there are several ways to offer the advice so it will be received by a man in a more positive light. This is true at home and at work.

Here are several ways for a woman to begin a sentence that makes unsolicited advice less demeaning for a man:

"I'm sure you already know this, but…"

"Would you do me a favor and …"

"If you are interested in hearing a different opinion …"

"You have probably already considered this, but just in case you haven't …"

These lead-in phrases allow a man to hear her advice without feeling as though she doesn't trust him. It is a way for him to "save face" and not automatically reject her advice.

Advice to Men

Realize that while you may feel annoyed by a woman giving you unsolicited advice, it is in her nature to try to help out, and it does not imply that she does not trust you or your abilities.

Advice to Women

Recognize that men, unlike women, are very sensitive to hearing unsolicited advice. In fact, they may reject your advice, just because they did not ask for it, even if it was great advice. Try to use the lead-in phrases above to avoid him rejecting you completely.

Insight #22:

How Could You?

When a woman asks a man a "How-could-you?" question such as, "How could you forget?" it usually means she is upset about something. She actually wants to better understand the situation and feels that her question is a harmless expression of her feelings. She most often will ask a "How could you" question rather than stating her negative feelings, "I am mad that you forgot."

Because women tend to speak more indirectly and men speak more directly, there is a difference in the message that is heard by a "How could you" question. While she is expressing negative feelings about a situation, he is feeling directly attacked. For men, a "How could you" question is derogatory, insulting and demeaning. While women think the question is harmless, for most men, this type of question means it is time for a fight.

Advice to Men

Recognize that her use of a "How could you" question is not intended as a direct attack on you. If you respond defensively, she will likely become even more upset. Instead, try to respond in a way that explains your situation and also lets her talk and express her negative feelings. If she feels you are listening and really care about her, she will be able to respond back to you in a positive way.

Advice to Women

Try to avoid all "How could you" questions and instead use direct statements. Instead of saying, "How could you do that?" try a more direct approach and say, "I don't like it when you do that." Men respond much better to direct statements and requests, than they do to "How could you" questions that they feel are very insulting.

Insight #23:

Be Back Later

What does "I'll be back later" really mean? When a man leaves and says he will *be back later*, he feels confident he has given his partner respect by assuring her of his return. However, when he says he will *be back later*, she mistakenly assumes he will be gone only a couple of hours. Her assumption of "later" meaning a couple of hours is because if she were planning to be gone all day she would say, "I will be gone all day." Because of this mis-communication, she may be very upset with him when he returns at the end of the day.

If she gets concerned (after 4-5 hours), she may be compelled to call him to make sure he is okay. What she says is, "Where are you? I thought you would be back by now." What she means/wants to say is, "I was worried about your safety because I assumed you were coming home in 2-3 hours and you have been gone 4-5 hours." What he hears is, "You are late and I am mad at you! You should never go anywhere for that long without me. You better get home now." Because of this mis-communication, he gets annoyed with her for checking up on him, and she gets annoyed with him for not coming home sooner.

To avoid hurt feelings all around, couples need to be very specific in their communication and ask for clarification on subjects like "*be back later.*"

Advice to Men

When you leave, give her the worst case scenario for your return. She would rather be happily surprised if you return sooner than expected versus being upset with you because you returned later than she expected.

Advice to Women

When he leaves, ask him if he can give you a more specific time of his return, just so you can plan your day and be home upon his return. Do not judge him for his time away. Just let him know you would like a general time so that you will not worry about him if he is late.

Insight #24:

Who Needs Reassurance?

Men and women have different emotional needs, which may at times be hard to understand. However, in order to build and maintain a healthy relationship, sometimes you have to give your partner things that may not make sense to you. An example of these different needs would be a man's need for acceptance and a woman's need for reassurance.

Reassurance is a primary emotional need for most women (not to be confused with a woman who is needy or clingy). When a woman is feeling stressed or overwhelmed, she may look to a man for reassurance. When a woman asks, "Does this dress make me look fat?" she is not asking for a literal or logical answer about her body size – she is asking for reassurance that she is still attractive. What she wants to hear is, "You look beautiful!"

When a man can support a woman by filling this emotional need and giving her the reassurance she craves, she will feel loved. If a woman asks, "Do you still love me?" she does not want to hear him say, "Well, I'm still with you, aren't I?" What she is really asking for is reassurance that he loves her more than ever.

Advice to Men

Do not use logic or reason to answer her questions – and try not to get frustrated if it seems like she needs "constant" reassurance. Just confirm to her she is beautiful and that you love her very much. When you are able to do this, you will score bonus points every time.

Advice to Women

Do not feel bad for wanting reassurance – just be sure to clearly communicate this need to your partner. If he gives you the wrong answer, do not take it personal. Say to him, "The answer I was really looking for was, 'You are beautiful, and I love you very much.'" After a few times of telling him what you want to hear, he will get the idea and begin to give you the reassurance you need.

Insight #25:

Who Needs Appreciation?

When a couple first starts dating she will compliment him on any little task he does. However, as time goes by, she may start slacking off on the compliments and pretty soon he feels as if she does not appreciate anything he does.

If he is not getting his needs met with the thanks he used to get, he will quickly lose his desire to do any more tasks. Without the appreciation, he will ultimately begin to do less and less. This is a bad cycle to get into, but easy to get out of once you recognize it.

Advice to Men

If you need more appreciation, gently remind her that it is easier for you to do things for her if she notices – and by noticing the small things, it motivates you to do bigger things in the future.

Advice to Women

To get him to do more, appreciate him for what he is currently doing. It works best when you mention his specific task, thank him for it, and follow it up with how it affects you in a positive way.

Insight #26:

Is Grumbling the Same as Resistance?

Sometimes men grumble when a woman asks them to do something.

When a man grumbles or groans, a woman hears him resisting her request. She mistakenly thinks either he resents doing the task she asked of him, or that he disagrees and may not do it at all. A woman then feels the need to convince him to do the task, which most likely will frustrate him because he hears it as nagging.

What a grumble really means is that a man has resistance to changing his focus from what he is currently doing to whatever she has asked him to do. Grumbling, groaning or growling are all ways that men use to <u>release their resistance</u>. It does not mean they are not going to do the task; it does not mean they do not want to do the task; it is just a process men go through to change their focus. Grumbling is a man's way to let off some steam so he can then refocus on the new task.

Advice to Men

If you find yourself grumbling, explain to her right away that you still intend to do the task. That way she can leave you alone and she will not feel obligated to explain in great detail <u>why</u> you should to the task.

Advice to Women

Recognize that grumbling does not mean resistance. After giving him a task, let him grumble. You should just walk away and assume he will complete the task. His grumbling will actually make him feel better, and perhaps he will complete the task sooner.

Insight #27:

Always or Never?

When a man hears a woman say, "You ALWAYS do this," or "You NEVER do that anymore," he may think to himself, "That is just not true."

Women have a tendency to over-generalize statements, using words like always and never. The use of these words is not meant to be taken literally, but more so used for emphasis and to express negative feelings. When a woman says, "You never take me out dancing," what she really means is, "It has been a long time since we went dancing and I would like to go this weekend."

The problem with using always and never is that men take them literally and then feel the need to defend themselves, which usually causes arguments. When he challenges her point and explains that they just went dancing six months ago, she feels that he is ignoring what she said and not really caring for her. She thinks she told him she wants to go dancing, while all he hears is he "never" did something that he knows he has done. This is an example of a mis-communication that can be avoided with a better awareness of our differences.

Advice to Men

Before you jump on the defense and disagree with her "always and never" statements, try to read between the lines. What is she really asking for? She says: never go dancing. She means: want to go dancing. Once you realize this form of communication, you can respond in a positive way making her happy, rather than getting defensive and making her more unhappy.

Advice to Women

Try to avoid using "always and never" statements. If you accidentally use one and he gets defensive, realize he is likely using a literal translation and trying to defend himself. Reword your statement as a direct request such as, "It has been a long time since we went dancing and I would like to go this weekend." Remember, men respond much better to direct requests than they do to indirect statements.

Insight #28:

Can She Handle the Truth?

When a woman asks another woman for an opinion about herself, she almost always gets a positive response. For example, "Do you think my new haircut is too short?" Another woman will answer with a positive comment, such as, "No, it is definitely not too short," or "It is short, but it looks really cute on you." Regardless of what they really think, women usually put a positive or feel-good spin on their answers. They do not do this to be untruthful; they do this to protect the feelings of the other person. It is just what women do.

On the other hand, men tend to answer questions directly, without regard to how it will make the other person feel. For example, "Is your haircut too short? Yes, I liked it better the other way." While their answer is honest, it does not always feel good to a woman who is used to hearing a positive spin.

Before she asks him a question, she needs to ask herself if she can handle the truth if it is negative, or does she just want a feel-good response.

Advice to Men

When a woman asks you a question, be careful how you answer. Even though she may ask for the truth, she may be expecting you to put a positive, feel-good spin on your answer. Be sensitive to her expectations and try not to answer with a blunt, negative comment.

Advice to Women

Remember that men are very direct, so do not ask the question unless you are prepared to handle a negative answer. Instead of getting mad at him when he gives you the wrong answer, modify your questions so you can get the positive feedback you want. For example, "My haircut is a little short, but I think it still looks good, don't you?" When he hears your reaction, he will be more inclined to agree with you, which will make you feel good. This is not about being dishonest; it is about choosing your words carefully to increase the happiness of both partners.

Insights into Dating

Insight #29:

Too Busy to Date?

You love your job and you are working more than ever. After work, you head to the gym for an hour of exercise, and then drag yourself home for dinner and sleep. You spend your weekends doing laundry, grocery shopping, visiting friends and trying to squeeze in a favorite activity like biking or sailing. You have an exciting life, but where is that special someone to share it with?

With schedules getting fuller and work hours getting longer, who has time to meet that special someone? Let alone go out on dates and build a relationship. Never fear, with today's dating climate changing, there are always ways to get things done faster – including meeting someone special.

Busy people need to use a variety of options – all at the same time – to increase their odds of meeting someone. Here are 5 ways to meet someone: online/internet dating, speed dating events, singles events, professional dating service, and getting the word out to friends and family.

Advice to Men

To increase your chances of meeting someone special, adjust your criteria. If it has been a while since you had a relationship, it might be a good idea to try a "different type" of person and a new venue to meet her.

Advice to Women

To reach your goal of finding someone special, you may need to go out of your comfort zone and travel to venues where available singles are gathering. Keeping your options open will increase your chances of meeting someone.

Insight #30:

Who Talked First?

Do you remember who spoke first when you met your partner? Generally speaking, the person who speaks first is the 'masculine energy' person in the relationship. The person who speaks first or approaches first is the "Pursuer."

Unfortunately in today's society, it is very common for women to be the pursuers. Women have been conditioned to have the mentality of "if you want something, go get it," and this includes trying to get men. Unfortunately, when a woman goes after a man she assumes the masculine role, and the man (by default) has to assume the feminine role in the relationship.

To start a relationship off on the right foot, the man should approach the woman first and he should be the one to speak first. For a healthy relationship, he needs to be the pursuer.

Advice to Men

Don't be shy! Women love a man with courage. Be brave and say "hello" to her first.

Advice to Women

Be patient and wait for him to make the first move. I know this is really hard to do, but it is worth it. However, while you are waiting for him to pursue you, you can flirt by looking directly at him and smile as much as you want.

Insight #31:

Do You Want a Man or a Boy?

When a woman really likes a man, she often does things to make him like her, too. She wants to make him happy and does this by trying to meet his needs. Unfortunately, with this behavior of "doing things" for him (ex. his laundry), she ends up "taking care" of him. In other words, she "mothers" him. This mothering behavior (putting his needs before hers) naturally causes him to do less because she is taking care of everything so he doesn't have to.

As a result, when a man does less (because she is doing it all), he ends up with child-like behavior; creating a pseudo-'mother/son' relationship. The end result of this destructive relationship is that he loses his attraction to her. Another problem is that eventually she will become resentful because she is doing too much and he is not doing enough.

Advice to Men

Don't get lazy and let her "take care" of you. It may feel good at first, but ultimately it will ruin your relationship. Stay in your masculine role and try not to assume the easy, child-like role as it will soon end the intimacy.

Advice to Women

Stop taking care of him. It may feel like you are showing him how much you care, but in the end it will backfire. You need to sit back and let him do the naturally masculine task of "doing" things for you. The feminine role is appreciating his actions, not taking the actions for him.

Insight #32:

Office Romance: Risky

Throughout the year, companies may host an office party, which means socializing with coworkers. Some may want to take office socializing to the next level – flirting or even dating. These people need to ask the question, "Are office romances worth the risk?" People always set out to act professionally at the office – however romance is not about being professional, it is very personal. Romantic decisions are not made with your head; they are made with your heart. Moreover, because your heart is involved, you may not make the best decisions in regards to your career.

How will your coworkers feel when they find out you are dating a colleague or even the boss? Even when you try to keep an office romance quiet, it does not stay quiet. With an office romance, you cannot act on impulse because public displays of affection at work make everyone very uncomfortable. Getting caught kissing in the office is a quick way to lose the respect of your coworkers. Or worse yet, lose the respect of management.

Advice to Men

Even though you may be very attracted to a coworker, try to remember all the areas where your romance could negatively affect your career. You may want to spend more effort looking for love outside the office.

Advice to Women

Relationships are hard and they can be even harder if you work with your new love. Your personal life should enhance your happiness, not negatively affect your career. Try to avoid falling for a coworker. Put some more time into your outside activities to find the man of your dreams.

Insight #33:

The Best 3 Months

When we start dating someone we really like, we mistakenly believe the good feelings will last forever. Having chemistry with this person causes the sparks to fly and we feel like we have finally met the "right one." After all, how could it feel so good if this person is not the right one?

When you have chemistry with someone, you can't deny the awesome way you feel when you are around them. The reason we feel so good is the result of chemistry or more accurately, chemicals, i.e. hormones. That is the good news. The bad news is that it usually only lasts about 3 months.

After three months of believing you have met Mr./Ms. Right, reality sets in and the rose-colored glasses start to come off. This is the time to really get to know this person - the good and the bad, and then decide if you are still as compatible as you believed. Remember, most healthy relationships are 33% chemistry, 33% compatibility and 33% good communication.

Advice to Men

Although she feels like Ms. Right at the beginning, she will eventually become human and she probably won't laugh at all your jokes. Give your relationship some time and see if you are willing to be in a real relationship with a real woman.

Advice to Women

Realize he may seem like the perfect Mr. Right, but don't start making wedding plans until you have dated seriously at least 3 months. Then look at him for who he really is, and not who you thought he was at the beginning.

Insight #34:

Relationship Progression

Men and women view the progression of a relationship in a very different way. Women in a new relationship tend to want to move up to the next level (get more commitment), as soon as possible. Women believe that if she is happy at the present level of her relationship, she will be even happier at the next level. So, if dating feels good, she believes being engaged must feel even better; if being engaged feels good, then being married must feel even better. She is always striving for the next level.

Oppositely, if a man is happy at the present level of his relationship, he wants to keep it right where it is. He feels if they move up to another level, there is a 50-50 chance he won't be as happy as he is now. Men believe that any time there is a change – in any area of his life – there is a chance he might feel worse and not better. His belief is: "If it's not broke, don't fix it." He is always striving to keep the relationship at the current level of happiness.

When it comes to moving forward in a relationship, there is a big difference between the beliefs of men and women. The important thing to keep in mind is that these differences in beliefs are not based on the individuals, but rather on the differences in the sexes, so don't take it personal.

Advice to Men

Understand it is natural for a woman to want to move forward in a relationship. She cannot completely open up to you until she feels you are also moving to the next level. This is just how woman are, so try talking to her about your concerns.

Advice to Women

Realize that it is a natural behavior in most men to drag their feet, and do not take it personally. Let him know you cannot fully enjoy your relationship until it progresses forward – but do not pressure him into moving or you may lose him.

Insight #35:

Perfect Wife Without a Ring?

During a new relationship a woman may become so attracted to a man that she already thinks of him as her future husband. If she believes he is Mr. Right she will want him to think she is Ms. Right. So, she starts acting like she is the "perfect wife" for him. She unselfishly tries to meet all his needs, i.e. cooks/cleans for him, plans all their dates around his favorite activities, ignores her friends to accommodate his schedule, and she may even offer to do his laundry. The message she is trying to send is, "See how great your life will be when we are married."

Unfortunately, the message he hears is, "She really enjoys taking care of me, so I do not have to do any work. Since she seems so happy doing this now as my girlfriend, I won't ever have to marry her."

This mis-communication is setting up unrealistic expectations for both partners.

Advice to Men

Realize if she is making your life seem too easy, it is not going to last. If she is doing all the work, she <u>is</u> expecting a marriage proposal.

Advice to Women

Do not act like the "perfect wife" until you have a ring on your finger. Act like a cherished girlfriend who deserves to be taken care of and treated with respect.

Insights into
Relationships

Insight #36:

How to Keep the Chemistry

In order to have a healthy, long-term relationship you need one partner with masculine energy (personality) and one partner with feminine energy. It is this opposite polarization of the sexes that causes the initial attraction between men and women; it is also what <u>maintains</u> the attraction/chemistry through the years.

Without this polarization, we can be "friends" with our partner, but the sexual attraction diminishes and eventually disappears completely. Without the polarization we end up with a roommate and not a lover.

Although you may not always understand the differences in the opposite sex, don't try to change your partner to be more like you. Celebrate and support the differences in the opposite sex; this is the foundation of a healthy, long-term relationship.

Advice to Men

Stay in your masculine role (protector/provider) and support her in her feminine role (receiver). Even if she tries to do her share and take care of you, let her know it makes you feel good to "take care" of her.

Advice to Women

Try to get out of the masculine role. Rather than doing things for him, relax and let him take care of you. By letting him do things for you and truly appreciating him for it, he will naturally find you more attractive.

Insight #37 :

Rules to Scoring Points

We all keep score, but with a very different set of rules.

Men believe they earn points based on the size of the action. If they do a nice "little" thing for her they get just a few points and if they do a nice "big" thing for her they have earned a whole lot of points. In a man's world, he could keep a woman happy by buying her a new car (thinking he's earned a lot of points) and then he doesn't have to do anything else for the rest of the year.

Women use the "one-point" method for keeping score. Regardless of the size of the action, a man only earns one point. In a woman's world, a "little" something every day (be it a flower, a love note, or a hug and kiss) means as much, and in some cases more, than a "big" something once in a while.

Advice to Men

It's important for a woman to feel special every day. You'll be more successful in making her happy by doing a nice "little" thing for her every day, along with the occasional nice "big" things.

Advice to Women

Realize that men are keeping score differently and appreciate him for both the big and little things he does. But, let him know he'll get more mileage out of doing the daily nice "little" things for you.

Insight #38:

How do YOU Score Points?

In a relationship, when he does something nice for her, he earns 1 "brownie" point. When she does something nice for him, she earns 1 "brownie" point. In a perfect world, the score would always be equal or close to it. Sounds fair, right? However, a man may quit trying to earn points (doing something nice) after he thinks he is ahead of her by about 3 points, but a woman may continue earning points until she is about 3,000 points ahead of him.

Once he is "up" 3 points (having done 3 nice things for her), he'll stop doing nice things until she takes her turn and does something nice for him. This way, he always keeps the score equal.

However, a woman keeps score to a much higher number, continuing to earn more and more points, figuring he will notice how nice she is being and he will then start reciprocating. As the imbalance of her 3,000+ points continues to grow, so does her resentment towards him. Unfortunately, since he believes in keeping the score equal all the time, he assumes she does the same. So, if she continues doing nice things for him, he figures he must have scored points somewhere along the way, or else she would stop doing nice things for him.

Advice to Men

If she is doing nice things for you, but you are sensing she is feeling resentful about it, ask her if the score is still equal or if you are way behind. Most men, over time, will be behind on points without ever knowing it. Ask her about this BEFORE she does too much and gets really mad at you.

Advice to Women

If the score gets unequal, tell him. Trying to guilt him into being nice by doing more nice things for him does NOT work. You have to communicate clearly what you need from him, and tell him that the score doesn't feel equal to you.

Insight #39:

Which One are You?

To have a healthy, romantic relationship you need for one partner to be masculine and one partner to be feminine. Do you know which you want to be? If you are not sure, ask yourself this question, do you want to be respected for your thoughts or cherished for your feelings? Most everyone wants to choose both, but that is not an option; you have to pick just one. Here is a clue: everyone is masculine at work (being respected for their thoughts), but everyone does not have to stay that way at home. Here is another clue: when you are stressed out, do you want to go inside your head and figure out your problems (masculine) or do you want to talk it out with friends (feminine)?

Every successful relationship has only one masculine and one feminine partner. This combination is necessary to create polarity and in turn create chemistry and intimacy.

Advice to Men

Realize she may be struggling to get back into her feminine energy when she gets home from her masculine job. To help this shift, ask her how and what she is feeling. Ideally, you will help her move from her masculine head (thinking) into her feminine heart (feeling) for a healthier relationship at home.

Advice to Women

It is important to know that you can shift roles when you come home. If you want your partner to be masculine, you must change into the feminine role. If you want him to support and care for you and your feelings, you must let him be masculine. That means respecting him for his thoughts and appreciating him for his actions, so that he is then able to cherish you and your feelings.

Insight #40:

Traits of Masculine and Feminine

There are two different roles in a healthy relationship. Since everyone acts masculine at work, we can have a hard time understanding what is naturally masculine and what is naturally feminine when we are outside of work. Here is a partial list:

MASCULINE Characteristics
- Has a narrow, direct focus
- Wants to protect and provide for your partner
- More in your head (thinking) rather than in your body (feeling)
- Wants partner to feel safe and secure – because of you
- Silently think about what is bothering you (do not talk about it)

FEMININE Characteristics
- Feels an instinctive need to talk about what is bothering you
- Able to freely express your emotions
- Wants to feel special – especially to your partner
- Wants to be cared for and respected for your feelings
- Wants to feel safe and secure

Advice to Men & Women

This partial list should help explain some of the differences in our natural traits or characteristics. While you may think it is just your partner who is different, it turns out it may be the entire opposite sex who is different from you.

Use this information to try to understand and appreciate your differences. These differences are sometimes frustrating, but they are ultimately the cause of the attraction and chemistry between partners.

Insight #41:

Happily Ever After. Really?

And they lived happily ever after – right?!

When a woman gets married (or moves in with her boyfriend), she believes her relationship will automatically get better (he will now give her more emotional support and meet more of her needs to make her happy).

However, when a man gets married (or moves in with his girlfriend), he believes he has finally "closed the deal" so the hard work is over and he can now relax (he can give her less emotional support and she will still be happy).

With these different expectations, it's no wonder so many marriages fail. But, with awareness of how the opposite sex has different expectations (not right vs. wrong, just different) it is possible to live happily ever after.

Advice to Men

If you want her to be happy, you need to realize you can NEVER quit giving her the support she needs. Just because she has committed to you, does not mean you get to stop listening and caring.

Advice to Women

Realize your man will NOT turn into Prince Charming just because he's wearing a wedding ring. You need to communicate clearly to him what your needs and expectations are before you get married (don't assume he already knows). Clear and direct communication will allow him to give you the support you need, so he can make you happy.

Insight #42:

How Strong is 'Feminine'?

Why do strong, independent women have to 'be feminine' to make their relationship work? A true feminine-energy woman has the ability to get her needs met, and that makes her strong.

Feminine does not mean weak and submissive. As most men already know, feminine energy is often much stronger than masculine. A feminine woman knows how to promote the masculine side of her partner so he feels strong and confident and he is then willing to give her what she needs to be happy. A feminine woman knows that there is no reason to argue with him, because she knows how to communicate in a way that supports both his and her needs – and she ultimately gets ALL her needs met.

Being feminine means she radiates energy and love. She is nurturing, not mothering. She is emotional, not whiny. She knows what she wants, and she asks her partner for it – she does not suffer in silence hoping her partner will read her mind and give her what she wants (that is the mothering trait a feminine woman tries to avoid). She knows her partner wants to make her happy and she supports him in this by telling him what she needs and appreciating him when he gives it to her.

Advice to Men

Support and encourage her to be feminine. Assure her that you want to make her happy and that she is beautiful when she radiates feminine energy.

Advice to Women

Realize you will get more out of your relationship if it is balanced. He will be better able to meet your needs if you stay in your feminine energy rather than competing with him to be masculine.

Insight #43:

Who is Caretaker of Your Relationship?

Have you ever wondered why women spend so much time talking about relationships, while men seem to rarely give it a thought?

Women are the "caretakers of the relationship." This happens naturally because women generally measure their own self-worth based on the strength of their personal relationships. Women take pride in being labeled a good wife, good mother or good daughter. However, men will base their self-worth on their career status and their ability to "get the job done." Men take pride in knowing they've done a good job at work or completed a difficult project.

Advice to Men

When she wants to talk about your relationship, you need to let her talk and give her support (tell her she's a good partner). Remember, what makes her feel good is when you give her reassurance that your relationship is doing well.

Advice to Women

Don't be offended if he isn't excited to talk about your relationship. Men equate talking about a relationship as needing to fix it and if he feels it isn't broke there is no need to fix it. Just because he may not want to talk about your relationship does NOT mean he doesn't care about it.

Insight #44:

Money vs. Love

We all have needs: physical needs (food, shelter, sex, etc.) and emotional needs (love, appreciation, understanding, etc.). Sometimes we get caught up in the false need to make more money, because we mistakenly believe our physical needs and wants are more important than our emotional needs. We think money will buy us happiness. Sure a new car with make you feel good, but the appreciation of a partner will feel even better and last longer.

While it is true money can help meet our physical needs, it cannot meet our emotional needs. In fact, working longer hours (to make more money) can make it harder to get our emotional needs met. Spending more time at the office means spending less time with our partner, who is usually the primary provider of our love, appreciation, understanding, etc.

Advice to Men & Women

Take a look at your life and see if you have a good balance between your work life and your personal life. It is crucial to put equal amounts of energy into meeting both physical needs and emotional needs.

Insight #45:

Is She Masculine at Home?

Every successful relationship has only one masculine energy partner and one feminine energy partner. This combination is necessary to create polarity and in turn create chemistry and intimacy.

There is a major problem in relationships today because as women become successful at work they become more masculine. Then when they come home from work, they may be unable to shed their masculine energy. When a woman stays masculine at home with her masculine partner, there are two possible outcomes. The first outcome is a situation where she is so powerfully masculine that he becomes more feminine to keep the energy in balance. Unfortunately, when a man becomes feminine, the woman begins to disrespect him and this causes problems.

The second outcome is when the woman is masculine but the man stays masculine. He will be in competition with her and he will not care for her or her feelings. She then resents him for arguing with her and not caring for her.

Either way, both partners lose. The best scenario is when a "feminine" woman allows a man to be his naturally "masculine" self. When this happens both partners are able to enjoy each other's qualities and support each other in a way that feels good for both partners.

Advice to Men

Stay masculine and support her in becoming feminine – even when she wants to be masculine.

Advice to Women

Leave your masculine energy at the office and change into your feminine energy at home. It feels good to have a man care for you.

Insight #46:

Emotional Support

Some times when a woman is feeling stressed and overwhelmed, she turns to her partner for support. Many times the kind of support he gives her is not the kind she needs. This results in her staying upset, and now he is also upset because he tried to help her and she still does not feel better.

When a woman has a problem, like not enough time to get her chores done, she may feel overwhelmed and express her frustration to her partner. He naturally wants to help her and make her feel better. He may say, "Don't worry about it; it will all get done eventually." What he means is that he wishes she would not get so upset over something he sees as a small and easily solved problem. What she hears is, "You have no reason to feel stressed, so get over it."

When she needs support, he needs to ask her what he can do to help her and reassure her that together they can solve her problem.

Advice to Men

Practice saying, "I'm here for you, and we will get this problem figured out." Remove from your vocabulary, "Don't worry about it." She will never feel better just by you telling her to stop worrying.

Advice to Women

When he tries to help, and it does not feel better, tell him what you really need to hear from him. Tell him you appreciate his efforts, but what will make you feel better is if he gives you hope that you can work together to solve the problem. You may even have to give him the exact words to use. This is okay, because he really does want to support you – and just may not know how to say it.

Insight #47:

Are you Being Taken for Granted?

At the beginning of a relationship, it is easy to give your partner your attention. His stories are interesting and her laughter is contagious. As time goes by something changes; conversations turn into "Yes, Dear," "Fine, whatever you say," and "The game is almost over, can it wait until then?" We have all heard the complaint, "I feel like I am being taken for granted."

To avoid the feeling of being taken for granted, couples need to realize the amount of "good stuff" they get from their partner is frequently related to the amount of attention they give to their partner.

Giving attention to your partner not only includes spending time with them, but also focusing on them and talking to them about what they are interested in (even if you have absolutely no interest in it). Giving undivided attention to your partner will make them feel good about themselves and in turn, they will want to make you feel good, too.

Advice to Men

You can still watch football without her, but when it is over focus your attention back on her. Ask her about her day and really listen. One of women's greatest needs is to be heard. Just listening is what will make her feel special.

Advice to Women

Even though you may have no interest in his latest project or hobby, take some time and ask him about it. Listen to him, without judging him. Giving him attention and even appreciation will make him feel so good he will want to give it back to you.

Insight #48:

Managing Money

What is the best way for a couple to manage money? Of course, most couples have their own opinion of what works best, but here is a tip. Money should be divided between his, hers and ours. This type of division works best for avoiding arguments on where the money should be spent.

It works like this: a portion or percentage of each person's paycheck goes into a joint account, which is used for household expenditures: bills, groceries, kid's clothes, etc. Then his leftover money (disposable income) goes into his personal account and her leftover money goes into her personal account. It is important for each person to have sole control over his or her personal spending money. The personal accounts are used for whatever each person wants, without the need for approval of their partner – which is how arguments are avoided.

When figuring your budget, keep in mind the traditional male in the relationship will be using his money for date night. Be sure to figure in extra budget money into his personal account for this reason. It makes him feel masculine to spend his money on her, and it makes her feel feminine to be treated to a date vs. just eating out because they were too tired to cook.

Advice to Men

If you make more money than she does, do not expect her to pay an equal amount into the joint account. You should each pay a percentage of your paycheck to make it fair.

Advice to Women

Insist on having your own spending money. It is a great feeling (a very feminine feeling) to know you can buy anything you want (just for you) and you don't need his approval. Whether your budget allows you to buy new shoes from Wal-Mart or from Macy's, it is still your money you are spending, just on you.

Insight #49:

When He Brings Work Home

There are times when a man's drive home is not long enough to shake off a bad day at work. When a man brings work home, it is not usually by choice and frequently involves him needing to solve a work problem. When a man has a specific problem to solve, he may not want to talk. If he is "processing" a problem in his head, he needs time alone. He may not need to be by himself, but he needs to be alone in his head. He may want to read the newspaper or watch TV, but he does <u>not</u> want to talk.

Unfortunately, most women interpret a man's silence as a signal for her to take control of the situation and find out what is bothering him – so she can help him fix it. This causes a bigger problem because her "help" is usually the last thing he wants.

Men process thoughts and problems quietly in their heads before they speak, while most women prefer to "talk out" their problems in order to find a solution. These different problem-solving styles need to be recognized and accepted in order to avoid making the problem worse.

Advice to Men

Tell her you need time alone to think – but reassure her you will discuss things with her as soon as you have finished processing your thoughts. It is also helpful to let her know it is a work issue, so she does not worry that your problem is with her and your relationship.

Advice to Women

Do <u>not</u> try to help him solve his problems. The best way to help him is to leave him alone with his thoughts. While you are waiting for him to finish processing, do something fun like calling a friend or reading a book.

Insight #50:

Where Did the Romance Go?

Ever wonder why he was so romantic in the beginning of your relationship, but not now?

There really is a good reason. When men are presented with a challenge, they focus on it until they have reached their goal or solved the problem. Then, feeling proud of their accomplishment, they sit back and relax; then move on to their next challenge. Unfortunately, many men look at relationships in this same manner. The woman he is dating is the challenge so he puts a lot of time, energy and focus into courting her until he has "won" her. Once he is confident that she is committed to him, he has reached his goal and can now sit back and relax.

What men do not realize is that women need romance all through the relationship, not just at the beginning. When a man stops the romance (which is something she needs), many times the woman will stop appreciating him (which is something he needs) and the relationship starts to decline. If his romantic behavior becomes stale or predictable, she cannot continue to be excited about being with him.

Advice to Men

You have the power to keep the love alive. Put more effort into romancing her even after you are in an exclusive relationship. Continue being romantic, i.e. spontaneity, flowers for no reason, planning dates, going out dancing. This type of romance will put the spark back in your relationship and she will respond with appreciation and receptivity.

Advice to Women

When you get settled in a relationship, don't settle down. Although it is easier to stay home and rent videos rather than going out to the movies, don't get lazy. Let him know you still need to have dates. Ask him to continue to plan your dates in advance and take you out on the town. You both need this. Keeping the romance alive will keep the relationship alive and healthy.

To get even more insights (an additional 50),
see Karen Card's next book in the series,

"How to Get EVEN MORE Love –
50 NEW Insights into the Opposite Sex"

About the Author

Karen Card, noted relationship expert and author, has helped hundreds of clients achieve happier and healthier relationships through her personalized coaching, books and seminars. Karen's respected reputation as the "go-to" relationship problem-solver – she boasts a 93% success rate – is owed to her dedication and individualized approach to each and every client.

Karen is the author of two other relationship books, "Get EVEN MORE Love – 50 NEW Insights Into the Opposite Sex"; and "MAN FACTS – 10 'Must Know' Secrets About Men". Her articles have appeared in numerous newspapers and magazines throughout the nation.

She offers one-on-one relationship coaching to clients throughout the United States, and regularly conducts workshops and teleseminars on a variety of relationship topics.

Karen Card, Relationship Expert
Coaching For Love
P.O. Box 4887
Clearwater, Florida 33758-4887
(727) 512-2899
Karen@CoachingForLove.com

Sign up for FREE relationship tips at
www.CoachingForLove.com

Made in the USA
Middletown, DE
22 January 2022